VIMY

100 YEARS

**MOLLY McCULLOUGH AND
MÉLANIE MORIN-PELLETIER**

**CANADIAN WAR MUSEUM
MUSÉE CANADIEN DE LA GUERRE**

Library and Archives Canada
Cataloguing in Publication

McCullough, Molly, author
Vimy: 100 years / Molly McCullough
and Mélanie Morin-Pelletier.

(Souvenir catalogue series, ISSN 2291-6385; 19)
Issued also in French under title:
Vimy : 100 ans.
ISBN 978-1-988282-06-0 (softcover)

1.   Vimy Ridge, Battle of, France, 1917 –
      Social aspects – Canada.
2.   Vimy Ridge, Battle of, France, 1917 –
      Influence.
3.   Memory – Social aspects – Canada
I.   Morin-Pelletier, Mélanie, author.
II.   Canadian War Museum, issuing body.
III. Title.
IV. Series: Souvenir catalogue series; 19.

D545.V5M23 2017
940.4'31
C2017-901050-6

Published by the
Canadian War Museum
1 Vimy Place
Ottawa, ON K1A 0M8
warmuseum.ca

Printed and bound in Canada

Cover image:
Shutterstock.com & 19920085-915,
George Metcalf Archival Collection,
Canadian War Museum

Souvenir Catalogue series, 19
ISSN 2291-6385

CONTENTS

FOREWORD

Over the course of four days in April 1917, close to 100,000 Canadian soldiers took part in a bloody battle that would come to symbolize Canada's participation in the First World War: the Battle of Vimy Ridge.

As gunners bombarded German troops with hundreds of thousands of shells, the Canadian infantry advanced on their adversary's positions, eventually capturing the ridge. The victory came at an enormous price, with 10,600 casualties, including close to 3,600 deaths.

One hundred years later, the Battle of Vimy Ridge continues to hold an important place in Canada's collective memory.

Today there are no surviving soldiers to share their experience of the battle or interpret its significance. Still, many Canadians think of Vimy when they envision the First World War.

This souvenir catalogue and the exhibitions it represents explore not just the attack on Vimy Ridge but also the century of commemoration that has followed, and how our perceptions of the battle have evolved over time.

Through years of retelling and commemoration, the battle has taken on greater symbolic significance, being commonly portrayed as a pivotal moment in Canada's emergence as a nation.

Four themes emerge: how commemoration contributes to **grieving** and **healing**; how individuals and groups **recognize** the contributions of others during wartime; the role of commemoration in strengthening the bonds of community and family and creating a sense of **belonging**; and how remembrance has been used to **promote** certain values and causes.

In addition to its vivid portrayal of a First World War milestone, *Vimy – 100 Years* provides a potent reminder that commemoration is a way of constructing the past and shaping our sense of national identity.

Stephen Quick
Director General
Canadian War Museum

INTRODUCTION

AFTER THE BATTLE, MEMORY REMAINS

One hundred years ago, Canadians fought a bloody battle at a place in France called Vimy Ridge. No one is alive today with direct memory of the battle — or even the war in which it was fought.

But Canadians continue to remember and commemorate the Battle of Vimy Ridge. We erect memorials, we tell and retell stories, we treasure keepsakes and we participate in public and private rituals.

Canadian troops fought many battles during the First World War, but today Vimy is the only one that many Canadians can name. It has been commemorated in monuments, souvenirs, textbooks, ceremonies and songs.

These commemorations have created powerful collective memories of Vimy Ridge that have made it a landmark in Canada's military history.

Vimy – 100 Years sheds light on how and why Canadians commemorate war by exploring private and collective memories of the Battle of Vimy Ridge, the First World War and more recent conflicts.

Painted by Captain William Frederick Longstaff
1929

VIMY: BATTLE AND MEMORIAL

The Canadian Corps captured Vimy Ridge from the Germans in April 1917 through brutal and costly fighting.

After the battle, and after the war, Canadians marked and honoured the terrible losses in numerous ways. The building of a grand national monument at Vimy Ridge was one of them.

THE CANADIAN CORPS

The Canadian Corps was Canada's primary fighting formation during the First World War.

By late 1916, the Canadian Corps consisted of four infantry divisions and support units of almost 100,000 soldiers. Soldiers and politicians demanded that the four divisions fight together in the Corps. The soldiers could get to know one another in a semi-permanent corps structure, and the hard lessons of battle would spread more easily from unit to unit.

THE CORPS COMMANDERS

Lieutenant-General Sir Julian Byng took command of the Canadian Corps in May 1916. Byng was much loved by his Canadian soldiers, who took pride in calling themselves the "Byng Boys." An experienced British cavalry general, he understood the importance of preparing his forces with intense training and in supporting them with massive firepower from artillery, mortars and machine guns.

Sir Julian Byng, on the left, speaks with Sir Arthur Currie, who replaced Byng as the Corps commander in June 1917.

⚐ MEDAL SET

Sir Julian Hedworth George Byng,
Field Marshal and Viscount Byng of Vimy,
G.C.B., G.C.M.G., M.V.O

THE SHIELD OF ARRAS
BEFORE THE BATTLE

Vimy Ridge was a geographical feature in northeastern France that had been held by the Germans since October 1914.

The ridge was known as the Shield of Arras, as it was close to the city of the same name, and bordered the valuable coalfields of Lens. Holding the ridge allowed the Germans to protect and mine the coal, an important source of energy in their war effort.

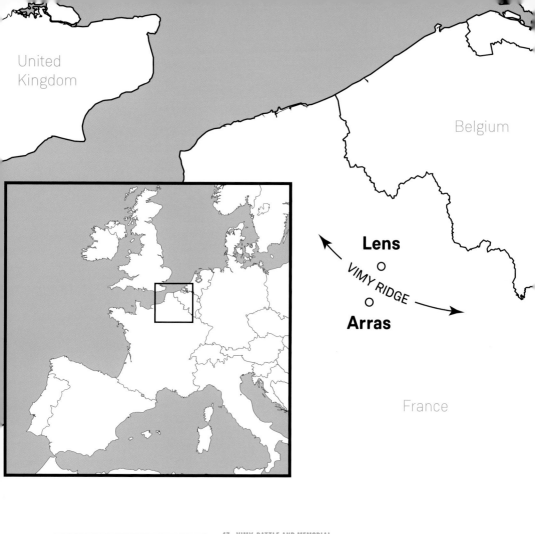

United Kingdom

Belgium

Lens

○

VIMY RIDGE

○

Arras

France

A SHATTERED LANDSCAPE

The French and the Germans had fought
multiple battles over Vimy Ridge during the
first two years of the war. The ground was
pitted with shell craters, underground tunnels
and rotting unburied corpses.

PREPARING FOR BATTLE

The Canadian Corps prepared thoroughly for the Battle of Vimy Ridge. The infantry went through a period of intense training, learning to fight together and practicing firing and coordinated movements on the battlefield.

Canadians built and repaired roads and rail lines, often under German artillery and mortar fire. They moved 1.6 million shells and thousands of tons of supplies to the forward positions to support the coming battle. They also dug or expanded 13 underground tunnels, some as long as 1,500 metres, to protect the infantry from enemy shellfire.

Canadian commanders and soldiers prepared for the coming battle with this relief map. A trench map was cut along the elevation contour lines and mounted on layers of cardboard to form a three-dimensional map of the ridge.

The Canadian objectives are shown with black, red, blue and brown lines. To the north of the ridge, the green line indicates the April 12, 1917 attack by the 4th Division against the German-held position known as the Pimple.

LEAD UP TO THE BATTLE

"At 8 a.m. a terrific bombardment started up. The roar was ear-splitting... Our troops are now raiding Fritzy two [or] three times every day [and] it is said the offensive is starting in a couple of days."

— Private William Antliff,
    No. 9 Canadian Field Ambulance, April 5, 1917

The artillery played a crucial role in the weeks before the battle by destroying enemy defences, harassing and killing German defenders, clearing barbed wire and suppressing enemy counter-battery fire.

NO MAN'S LAND

No Man's Land, the ground between opposing army trenches, was a dangerous place. The risk of being hit by a sniper or machine gun fire, or running into an enemy trap, was always present.

A Franciscan friar gave this rosary to Private John Whitton when he was recovering from wounds sustained while patrolling No Man's Land two days before the attack on Vimy Ridge. Although wounded in the head, Whitton eventually returned to the battlefield and fought to the end of the war.

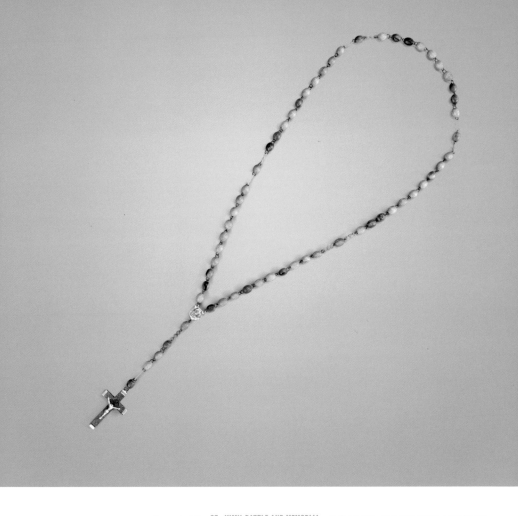

THE BATTLE OF VIMY RIDGE

The Battle of Vimy Ridge was fought from April 9 to 12, 1917. Close to 100,000 Canadian troops and more than 30,000 British gunners used innovative tactics to capture the heavily fortified ridge from the German army.

British and Canadian gunners methodically fired hundreds of thousands of shells to assault enemy fortifications and provide a moving bombardment known as a creeping barrage. The Canadian infantry used the creeping barrage as a shield to cover its advance toward the German positions.

Whenever they encountered enemy strongholds, Canadian machine gunners, bombers and riflemen pinned down the German defenders, while others rushed in to kill or capture them.

Success came at a heavy cost. Of the 10,600 Canadian casualties, nearly 3,600 died.

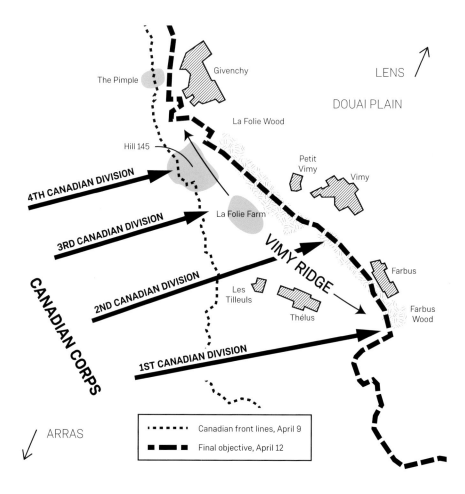

The Pimple

Givenchy

LENS

DOUAI PLAIN

La Folie Wood

Hill 145

4TH CANADIAN DIVISION

Petit Vimy

Vimy

3RD CANADIAN DIVISION

La Folie Farm

CANADIAN CORPS

VIMY RIDGE

Farbus

2ND CANADIAN DIVISION

Les Tilleuls

Thélus

Farbus Wood

1ST CANADIAN DIVISION

ARRAS

···· Canadian front lines, April 9

▬ ▬ Final objective, April 12

This battlefield map shows where the four Canadian infantry divisions attacked Vimy Ridge. The 1st Division fought over relatively flat ground and advanced the farthest, gaining over 4 kilometres. The other divisions progressed up the steep ridge, with the 4th Division, on the far north, assaulting the heights of Hill 145. On April 12, the 10th Canadian Infantry Brigade successfully assaulted the German position known as the Pimple.

Official war artist Richard Jack's painting captures Canadian gunners firing round after round towards Vimy Ridge.

THE TAKING OF VIMY RIDGE, EASTER MONDAY, 1917

Painted by Richard Jack
1919

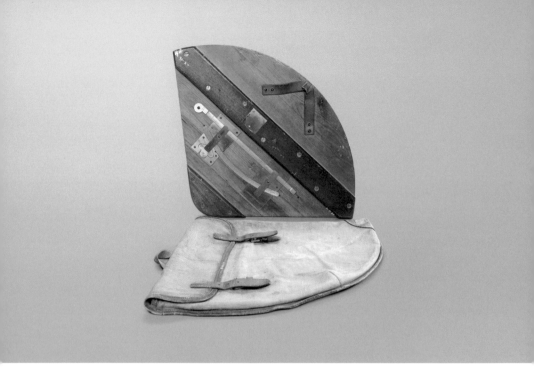

SCIENTIFIC GUNNERY

Soldiers used sophisticated technology during the Battle of Vimy Ridge to locate, harass and destroy enemy artillery guns. This plotting board and artillery telemeter were among the tools used to measure distances to enemy guns, identify their locations and then direct the Allied guns to smash the targets.

⚑ **FIELD ARTILLERY PLOTTING BOARD
AND ARTILLERY TELEMETER, MK IV**

LEWIS MACHINE GUN

The Lewis machine gun was one of the most important weapons of the war. Able to fire hundreds of bullets per minute, the Lewis was the infantry's primary light machine gun and increased a unit's firepower.

NEWLY WON TERRITORY

The Vimy-Liévin Line was a series of German defensive positions. By the end of the battle, the Germans had retreated from the ridge and their trenches. The Canadians put up this sign to indicate their newly won territory.

A STRETCHER BEARER

This uniform was worn by stretcher bearer John Russell Clark during his service at the front. Clark served with the 13th Field Ambulance at Vimy Ridge. His diary on April 9, 1917 reads: "Terrible number of wounded. At one time, nearly 500 lying on stretchers in open."

A CANADIAN VICTORY IN A FAILED CAMPAIGN

The Battle of Vimy Ridge was part of a larger Franco-British campaign. While the British initially made gains, they suffered 159,000 casualties over the next 39 days in the Arras region.

The main French offensive failed and was suspended in May 1917. After tremendous losses, thousands of French soldiers mutinied and refused to enter the line again. It was months before the French recovered.

⚑ **BRITISH GUNNERS IN ACTION**

Battle of Arras
April 1917

REMEMBERING THE WAR

Starting during the First World War, individuals, communities and nations found different ways of commemorating contributions to the war effort.

After the war, community memorials were built across the country. The government recognized the personal losses of Canadian families with official honours, and national loss with memorials in Ottawa and on former battlefields overseas.

THE CANADIAN NATIONAL VIMY MEMORIAL

A British committee assigned Canada eight battle sites to commemorate. Canada chose Vimy Ridge as the location for its most prominent overseas memorial.

In 1920, Toronto sculptor Walter Allward won the architecture competition for the national memorial. The jury selected his design from 160 submissions.

His winning design focused on the sacrifices and contributions of Canadians during the First World War.

The memorial was unveiled in July 1936.

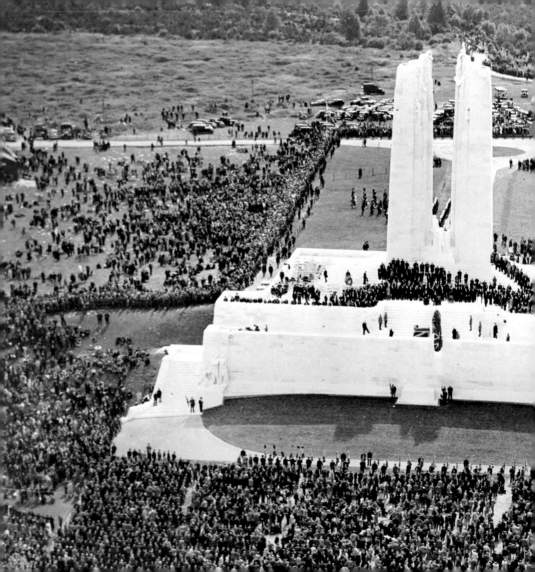

GRIEVING AND HEALING

After a war, we remember those who died. Private and public commemorations help us grieve and heal.

⚑ CROSS THAT MARKED THE GRAVE
OF LIEUTENANT NORMAN PAWLEY,
WHO DIED AT VIMY RIDGE

AN UNCONVENTIONAL GRAVESTONE

In this image, Daisie Lawledge Evans points to her brother's name on the Vimy Memorial. Private Walter Elliott Lawledge was killed at the Battle of Vimy Ridge.

The names carved on the base of the memorial do not represent those killed during the Battle of Vimy Ridge. They commemorate the 11,285 Canadians killed in battles throughout France during the war whose bodies were never recovered.

The Imperial War Graves Commission proposed carving the names on the Memorial to take the place of traditional gravestones and help families grieve.

SORROW AND SACRIFICE

Many First World War commemorations equated death in war with sacrifice. This association reassured some survivors and family members that their loved ones had died for a reason.

"HE DIED FOR FREEDOM AND HONOUR"

Annie Lawledge received commemorative items after her son, Private Walter Elliott Lawledge, was killed at Vimy Ridge.

Official Memorial Plaques bore the names of the members of British Empire forces who died as a result of the First World War. The inscriptions on these commemorations present the deaths in terms of duty and sacrifice.

Annie Lawledge displayed her son's Memorial Plaque with his service medals.

"THEY DID THEIR DUTY WELL"

Dear Mrs. Coleman,

You have no doubt been informed of the death of your dear son Gunner C. J. Coleman. He and his comrades have done magnificent work and to them is due in part the great victory won on Vimy Ridge. They did their duty well, and we are all proud of them.

Sincerely Yours,

Hon. Capt. S Wilkinson
Chaplain

Chaplain Captain Samuel Wilkinson chose these words to provide comfort in this letter to Jenny Coleman, mother of Gunner Cyril James Coleman. Wilkinson focused on her son's duty and role in the Battle of Vimy Ridge.

Many chaplains, nurses and soldiers wrote letters to the families of those killed. They often provided a soothing narrative of the soldiers' final days that explained their deaths as a sacrifice for Western civilization and Christianity.

Between 1914 and 1917

A MOTHER'S SACRIFICE

This Cross is presented to you in memory of one who in the Great War, died for King and Country.

— Message on First World War Memorial Cross card, Minister of Militia and Defence

Mary Churchill displayed her Memorial Cross on her son's portrait. Lieutenant Alfred Snow Churchill died at the Battle of Vimy Ridge.

The Memorial Cross, issued by the Canadian government, presents mothers' and wives' losses in terms of sacrifice. It suggests that women gave up their loved ones for a great and noble cause. It is still awarded today.

HEALING RITUALS

At home and overseas, Canadians coped with loss through commemorative rituals.

Saying a proper goodbye was important enough to servicemen and women that they erected grave markers and performed funeral ceremonies under difficult conditions.

Survivors may have taken comfort knowing that their friends would give them a funeral if they were killed.

September 1917

This wooden cross marked the grave of Private John Firman Ashe, killed during the Battle of Vimy Ridge. It was assembled and placed on the grave by soldiers serving with a Graves Registration Unit.

Few examples of these wartime crosses have survived. Private Ashe's great-nephew, Jim Landry, inherited this one.

FINDING WAYS TO GRIEVE

During the First World War, families on the home front could not hold traditional burial services, because the bodies of their loved ones were not returned to Canada.

As a result, people performed other rituals to mourn the dead. In this photograph, Japanese Canadians gather in Vancouver around 1918 to mourn the death of Private Toshitaka Ishihara during the First World War.

The banner reads "In memory of Toshitaka Ishihara, who died as a soldier."

Private Charles Paul Crofoot's family requested a photograph of his grave marker in France. Crofoot was killed at the Battle of Vimy Ridge on April 12, 1917.

For families who could not travel overseas to visit their loved ones' graves, a picture of the grave marker could help provide some closure.

⚑ PRIVATE
CHARLES PAUL CROFOOT

Between 1914 and 1917

Director of Graves Registration & Enquiries.

Begs to forward as requested a Photograph of
the Grave of :—

Name *Crofoot*

Rank and Initials *Pte. C.P.*

Regiment *44. Canadian Inf.*

Position of Grave *Villers Station Mil.*
7.f.21 *Cemetery*

Nearest Railway Station *Villers-au-Bois*

All communications respecting this Photograph should quote
the number (*21/658*) and be addressed to :—
Director of Graves Registration and Enquiries,
War Office,
Winchester House,
St. James's Square,
London, S.W., 1.

Owing to the circumstances in which the photographic work is carried
on, the Director regrets that in some cases only rough Photographs can
be obtained.

"COPYRIGHT FULLY RESERVED."

LAVAL LIBERTY
HIGH SCHOOL
3PPCLI

WE REMEMBER THOSE
WHO HAVE FALLEN
AND THOSE WHO STILL
STAND. THANK YOU
TO THOSE WHO HAVE
GIVEN THEIR LIFE IN
SERVICE OF THEIR
COUNTRY.

RECOGNIZING WARTIME CONTRIBUTIONS

After a war, we select the stories we tell. We commemorate the events that have meaning for us and recognize the roles that people have played.

⊨ **WREATH HONOURING THE SERVICE OF THE 3RD BATTALION OF PRINCESS PATRICIA'S CANADIAN LIGHT INFANTRY**

2010

TO THE VALOUR OF THEIR COUNTRY-
MEN IN THE GREAT WAR AN
MEMORY OF THEIR SIXTY TH
DEAD THIS MONUMENT IS
BY THE PEOPLE OF

TO THOSE WHO SERVED

To the valour of their countrymen in the Great War and in memory of their sixty thousand dead this monument is raised by the people of Canada.

— Inscription on the Canadian National Vimy Memorial

Unveiled in 1936, the Canadian National Vimy Memorial recognizes the contributions of all the men and women who served during the First World War, and commemorates the more than 66,000 Canadians who died.

Here, a Canadian Women's Army Corps member reads the inscription on the Vimy Memorial during the Second World War.

HOLDING ON TO REMINDERS

"Goggles worn by me with a cracked lens, when I crashed in a shelled area near Vimy Ridge."

— Lieutenant Harold Molyneux, 1977

Men and women in the service brought home souvenirs of wartime experiences they wanted to remember.

These goggles reminded Lieutenant Harold Arthur Sydney Molyneux of his narrow escapes at Vimy Ridge.

As a soldier with the 75th Battalion, Molyneux was wounded during the Battle of Vimy Ridge.

He later transferred to the Royal Flying Corps and survived a plane crash in the Vimy area.

For almost 60 years, Molyneux kept the goggles he was wearing when he crashed. He eventually donated them to the Canadian War Museum.

A CANADIAN FLAG AT VIMY

Private James Davidson of the 5th Battalion carried this pre-war Canadian Red Ensign during his service on the Western Front. He had it with him at Vimy Ridge. The flag came from his home in Crescent Hill, Saskatchewan, and was given to him by his mother for good luck. After the war, Davidson brought the flag back to Canada.

BUILDING MEMORIES

Thousands of communities across Canada built monuments and other commemorative structures to recognize their citizens' contributions to the First World War.

This stained-glass window featuring the Vimy Memorial honours Canadians who died in action. It was installed in the University of Toronto's Soldiers' Tower in 2005.

Built in the 1920s, the tower initially commemorated members of the University of Toronto community killed during the First World War. It has since been rededicated to recognize the 1,185 university community members who died in both World Wars.

SOLDIERS' TOWER

1924

AWARDS

The British government awarded honours to many Canadian soldiers. Traditionally, military honours recognize particular types of actions, such as those demonstrating bravery and leadership.

Lieutenant-Colonel Thain MacDowell received the Victoria Cross, the British Empire's highest award for bravery, for his actions during the Battle of Vimy Ridge.

MacDowell, with the assistance of two runners, captured two German officers, 75 men and two machine guns. His battalion was then able to take its objective.

⚑ **MEDAL SET**

Lieutenant-Colonel Thain Wendell MacDowell, V.C., D.S.O.

British war artist Harold Knight painted this portrait of Lieutenant-Colonel Thain MacDowell. The values embodied by recipients of the Victoria Cross were held in such high esteem that the Canadian War Memorials Fund commissioned war artists to paint portraits of those honoured.

⚑ **MAJOR T. W. MACDOWELL, THE VICTORIA CROSS**

Painted by Harold Knight
Around 1918

ARTISTIC EXPRESSION

People often recognize wartime contributions through artistic expression.

The pictographs on this calfskin robe depict Corporal Mike Mountain Horse's First World War exploits. Mountain Horse was a soldier from the Kainai (Blood) reserve in Alberta.

The robe features 12 wartime experiences selected by Mountain Horse, and painted in the Niisitapiikwan (Blackfoot) warrior tradition by Ambrose Two Chiefs. Mountain Horse arranged the experiences in order of their importance to him.

BELONGING

After a war, families, communities and societies often feel the need to gather and renew the ties that bind them together. Commemorative gatherings and rituals give us a greater sense of belonging.

 *UNVEILING VIMY RIDGE MONUMENT*

Painted by Georges Bertin Scott
1937

A VIMY PILGRIMAGE

Eighteen years after the end of the First World War, thousands of war veterans returned to the French and Belgian battlefields where they had fought. Accompanying them were the widows and children of many of those killed. The tour culminated on July 26, 1936 with the unveiling of the Vimy Memorial, Canada's First World War memorial.

Participants described the journey as a pilgrimage. Veterans reunited with wartime friends to honour those killed and to remember shared suffering. Family members saw where loved ones lived, fought and, in some cases, died.

PILGRIMAGE WEAR

Vimy pilgrims wore berets adorned with patches and buttons identifying the group with which they were travelling, or their First World War military units.

SILVER PILGRIM MEDAL

Leonard Charles Evans, a Canadian
First World War veteran, received this
medal when he made the 1936 Vimy
pilgrimage. The Canadian Legion
issued a silver medal to all pilgrims.

Leonard Evans was accompanied by his wife, Daisie Lawledge Evans.

🏳 DAISIE AND LEONARD EVANS

During the 1936 Vimy pilgrimage

NEW GENERATIONS OF PILGRIMS

"I didn't know when I would have another opportunity to be part of such a huge commemorative event, for such a significant part of Canada's history."

— Ashlee Beattie, 2016

Since 1936, many Canadians have travelled to the Vimy Memorial.

Ashlee Beattie visited Vimy to participate in the 90th anniversary of the Battle of Vimy Ridge with friends who had similar interests and experiences. Ashlee had worked as a guide at Vimy Ridge the previous year.

This photo shows Ashlee (centre) with John and Lois Newell at the Vimy Memorial. John Newell attended the monument's unveiling as a boy and wore the 1936 pilgrim's medal when he returned in 2007.

A TOAST TO REMEMBER

The Canadian Corps Cyclist Battalion Association saved this bottle of champagne to commemorate its members' shared service during the First World War.

Starting in the 1930s, the members raised the unopened bottle at reunions, saluting their battalion and those who had died. They pledged that the final two surviving members would drink the champagne. In 1992, Wilfred D. Ellis, age 96, and William J. Richardson, age 98, uncorked this bottle to toast the battalion's memory.

A SEA OF POPPIES

Around five million people visited the commemorative art installation *Blood Swept Lands and Seas of Red* at the Tower of London in 2014.

Between July 17 and November 11 of that year, artists Paul Cummins and Tom Piper filled the Tower's moat with 888,246 ceramic poppies: one for each member of the British Empire forces killed during the First World War.

Marking the war's centenary, the installation attracted people who wanted to experience, and help create, a meaningful commemorative event.

TOWER OF LONDON POPPY

This ceramic poppy was part of the art
installation at the Tower of London. All
of the poppies were sold, raising millions
of dollars for charity.

PROMOTING A CAUSE

After a war, the stories we tell help us create a collective memory that we use to promote certain values and causes.

CONSTRUCTING MEMORY

The figures on the Vimy Memorial, such as the ones on the following page, promote a particular vision of Canada's First World War experience.

Some figures such as *Hope*, *Faith*, *Justice*, *Charity*, *Honour* and *Peace* represent the values for which Canadians fought the First World War.

⚑ *JUSTICE*

CANADA ON THE INTERNATIONAL SCENE

Max Aitken (later Lord Beaverbrook) started the
Canadian War Memorials Fund in 1916 to document
and promote Canada's war efforts.

The resulting paintings were used to publicize Canada's
contribution to a global war. They were displayed in
Canada and abroad, most notably at a Canadian War
Memorials exhibition in London, England in 1919.

This painting by Canadian official war artist A. Y. Jackson
highlights the Pimple, a German stronghold at the northern
tip of Vimy Ridge that was seized by the Canadians.

Jackson's work suggests that taking the hill was a
significant Canadian achievement. The catalogue
for the 1919 London exhibition explains the location's
significance: "Its tactical importance was such that its
capture became essential as soon as the ridge itself
had fallen to the victorious Canadians."

 *THE PIMPLE, EVENING*

Painted by A. Y. Jackson
1918

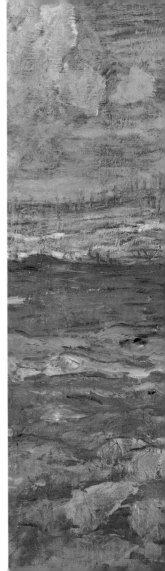

CONSIDERING POSTERITY

"I think it unfair to future citizens of Canada, to Canada's war effort and to myself to have that portrait handed down to posterity as a likeness of the Canadian Corps Commander."

— General Sir Arthur Currie, 1924

British war artist Sir William Orpen painted this portrait of General Sir Arthur Currie, who commanded the 1st Canadian Division at the Battle of Vimy Ridge.

Currie understood that commemorative paintings endorsed a particular image of Canada. He disliked this portrait, stating that it promoted a poor image of him as a military commander, and therefore of Canada's war effort. At his request, Orpen's painting was removed from the Canadian War Memorials exhibition at the National Gallery of Canada in 1924.

⚑ *LIEUTENANT GENERAL SIR ARTHUR CURRIE, GCMG, KCB*

Painted by William Orpen
1919

ACTIVISM

"I served my country. You've taken everything away from me... What [is] the good of my medals?"

— Sergeant Masumi Mitsui, 1942

People use the past to influence their future. Commemorations often figure in community struggles for social justice and change.

Sergeant Masumi Mitsui, shown here holding a First World War photograph of himself, protested against the forced relocation of Japanese Canadians during the Second World War by throwing his medals down in front of an internment official.

In 1942, Mitsui's family was split up and compelled to relocate. The government seized and sold his farm and most of his possessions.

Sergeant Mitsui fought at the Battle of Vimy Ridge, and distinguished himself at Hill 70 in August 1917. His medals commemorated his First World War service. He did not wear them publicly again until the 1980s.

FIGHTING TO BE A PART OF CANADIAN SOCIETY

They were considered good enough to fight for Canada; they certainly should be entitled as Canadian citizens to use the franchise.

— *Victoria Times*, April 1, 1931

The Japanese Canadian War Memorial in Vancouver, British Columbia bears the names of all community members who fought. It was a conscious effort to promote the community's participation in Canadian society, and thereby win the same rights as other Canadians.

⚑ JAPANESE CANADIAN WAR MEMORIAL

Stanley Park, Vancouver, B.C., 1920

In the early 20th century, Japanese Canadians did not have the right to vote. This right was first granted to Japanese Canadian veterans in British Columbia in 1931, but other Japanese Canadians had to wait until 1949.

More than 200 Japanese Canadians served in the First World War. Many fought at the Battle of Vimy Ridge. The Japanese Canadian War Memorial was unveiled on April 9, 1920, the third anniversary of the beginning of that battle.

PROMOTING NATIONAL VALUES

Over the past century, Canadians have used the Vimy Memorial in propaganda to define and promote national values.

This Second World War poster encouraged Canadians to support the war effort by invoking the memory of those who fought and died in the First World War. The Vimy Memorial was presented as a symbol of hope, determination and victory, urging Canadians to keep fighting during the Second World War.

THE TORCH; BE YOURS TO HOLD IT HIGH!
IF YE BREAK FAITH WITH US WHO DIE
WE SHALL NOT SLEEP, THOUGH POPPIES GROW
IN FLANDERS FIELDS.

McCRAE.

BIRTH OF A NOTION

"Vimy was more than a battle. It is a symbol of the coming of age of Canada as a nation, a nation which was brought to birth in emotion and feeling, and in a unity sealed by blood. May we always keep that feeling of togetherness and unity in this country."

— Lester B. Pearson, First World War veteran and Prime Minister of Canada, 1967

The notion of Vimy as a nation-building event first appeared in the 1960s. Since then, many Canadians have described the Battle of Vimy Ridge as the "birth of a nation." The repetition of this phrase is itself a commemoration that promotes the idea of a Canada that was united, independent and born on a First World War battlefield.

Initially voiced by politicians and veterans, the "birth of a nation" commemoration of the battle is now a part of Canadian popular culture.

⚑ PRIME MINISTER LESTER B. PEARSON
1963

CONTRIBUTIONS

We would like to thank the core members of the Vimy exhibition teams: Tim Cook, Krista Cooke, Marie-Louise Deruaz, Eric Fernberg, Patricia Grimshaw, Julie Savard and La Bande à Paul. We also want to recognize the invaluable contribution of many colleagues at the Canadian War Museum and the Canadian Museum of History: Fiona Anthes, Maggie Arbour, Mona Ardestani, Stacey Barker, George Barnhill, Ashlee Beattie, Andrew Burtch, Nic Clarke, Arlene Doucette, Tim Foran, Shirley Lam, Anne Macdonnell, Meredith MacLean, John Maker, Jeff Noakes, Sandra O'Quinn, Carol Reid, Susan Ross, Jessica Shaw, Joanne Stober and Lindsay Towle. The project also benefitted greatly from the expertise of Caroline Dromaguet, Tony Glen, Peter MacLeod and James Whitham. Special thanks are due to photographer Bill Kent and to publications coordinator Lee Wyndham for their excellent work in producing this catalogue.

PHOTO CREDITS

CANADIAN WAR MUSEUM

EXTERNAL SOURCES